Character Education

Forgiveness

by Lucia Raatma

Consultant:
Madonna Murphy, Ph.D.
Professor of Education
University of St. Francis, Joliet, Illinois
Author, *Character Education in America's
Blue Ribbon Schools*

Bridgestone Books
an imprint of Capstone Press
Mankato, Minnesota

Bridgestone Books are published by Capstone Press
151 Good Counsel Drive, P.O. Box 669, Mankato, Minnesota 56002
http://www.capstone-press.com

Library of Congress Cataloging-in-Publication Data
Raatma, Lucia.
    Forgiveness/by Lucia Raatma.
      p. cm.—(Character education)
      Includes bibliographical references and index.
      Summary: Explains the virtue of forgiveness and gives tips on how to practice forgiveness
in your home, school, and community.
      ISBN 0-7368-1132-X
      1. Forgiveness—Juvenile literature. [1. Forgiveness.] I. Title. II. Series.
BJ1476 .R32 2002
179′.9—dc21
                                                                                    2001003432

Editorial Credits
Sarah Lynn Schuette, editor; Karen Risch, product planning editor; Jennifer Schonborn,
    cover production designer and illustrator; Alta Schaffer, photo researcher

Photo Credits
Billy Graham Center Archives, Wheaton, Ill., 18
Capstone Press/Gary Sundermeyer, cover, 4, 6, 8, 10, 12, 14, 16, 20

1 2 3 4 5 6 07 06 05 04 03 02

Table of Contents

Forgiveness

Everyone makes mistakes. Forgiveness means accepting the mistakes others make. It also means asking for forgiveness when you make mistakes. It can be hard to forgive. You may feel angry. Forgiveness can help heal hurt feelings.

Practicing Forgiveness

Forgiveness can take a long time. Maybe someone broke your toy. You may be angry. The first step is to accept that your toy is broken. Next, tell the person how sad you are. Give them a chance to apologize. Then, try to forgive the person.

apologize
to say that you are
sorry about something

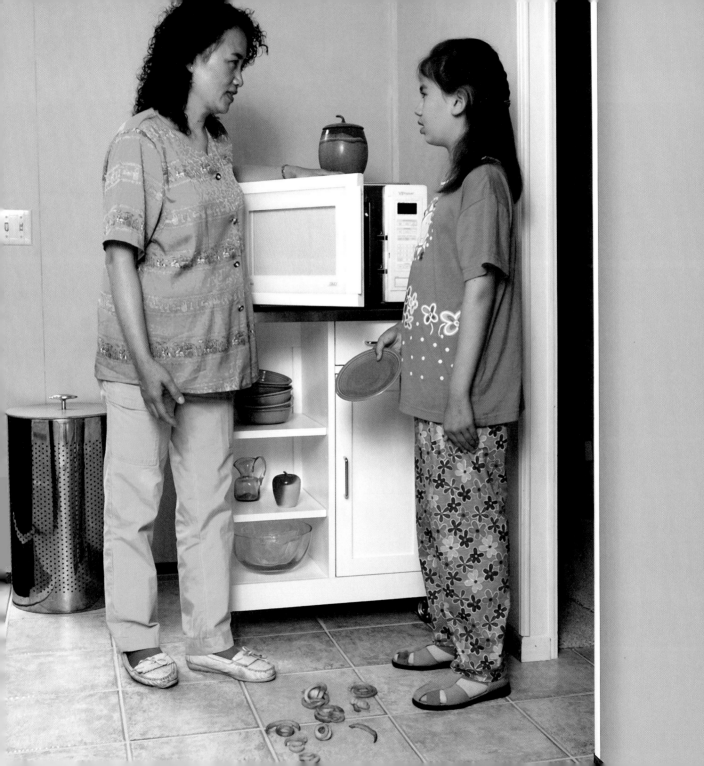

Asking for Forgiveness

You should take responsibility for the mistakes you make. Ask for forgiveness when you do something wrong. Apologize when you drop food on the floor. You can offer to clean it up.

responsibility

a duty or a job; responsible people follow rules and admit their mistakes.

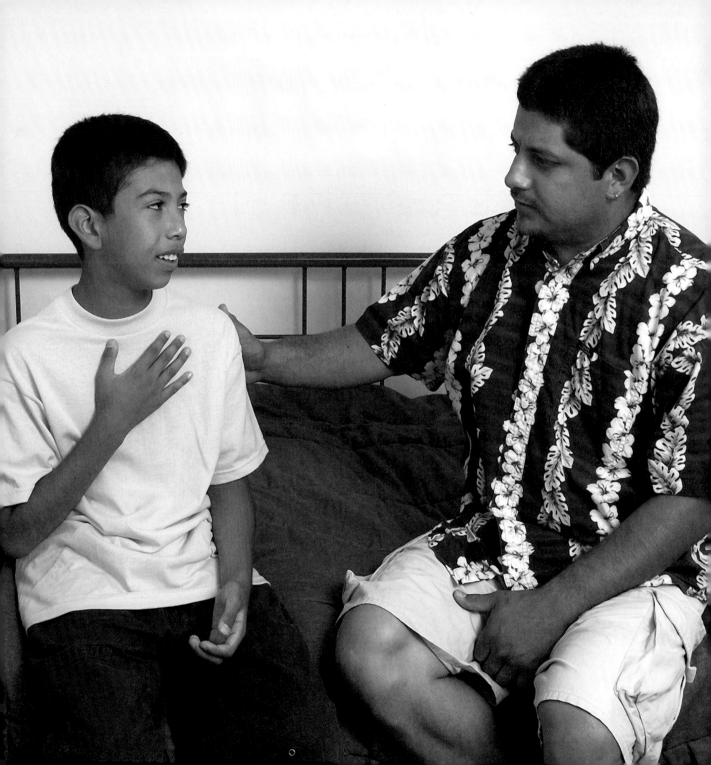

Forgiveness and Your Family

People in your family sometimes may disappoint you. They might be late to your baseball game. Tell your family members that you were disappointed. Let them explain why they were late. Try to forgive your family for being late.

disappoint

to let someone down by not doing what was expected

Forgiveness and Your Friends

Your friends also need your forgiveness. You may be angry because your friend lost your favorite yo-yo. Look for the yo-yo together. Your forgiveness gives your friend a chance to do better next time.

Forgiveness at School

Being teased at school can be hard. A classmate may call you names. Tell the classmate you do not like to be teased. Talk to a teacher if you need help. Try to forgive your classmate's actions. People who forgive do not hold grudges.

grudge
anger toward someone who has hurt or teased you in the past

Forgiveness in Your Community

You sometimes need to forgive people in your community. Maybe someone ran over your ball. You may get angry. But you can control your anger. Try to understand that accidents happen.

accident

something that is not intended to happen

"Forgiveness is an act of the will, and the will can function regardless of the temperature of the heart."

—Corrie ten Boom (pictured on right)

Corrie ten Boom

Corrie ten Boom lived in Holland during World War II (1939–1945). Corrie and her family were sent to a prison camp. Later, Corrie forgave the people who ran the camp. She then spoke to people all over the world. She asked them to forgive their enemies.

prison camp

a place where some people were forced to live and work during World War II; many people died in prison camps.

19

Forgiving Yourself

Forgiveness can make you feel better. Maybe you said hurtful things to a friend and you apologized. Your friend forgave you. But you may still feel bad. Give yourself a chance to do better the next time. Learn to forgive yourself when you make mistakes.

Hands On: Make Forgiveness Cards

It is important to forgive other people. But it is important to ask for forgiveness too. Saying "I am sorry" may help others forgive you.

What You Need
Construction paper
Markers
Crayons

What You Do
1. Think of someone you hurt or made angry. Decide to say you are sorry.
2. Fold one piece of construction paper in half to make a card.
3. Using crayons or markers, draw a picture on the front of the card. It could be a vase that you broke. Or you could draw yourself looking sad.
4. Write a note inside the card. Say you are sorry and ask for forgiveness.
5. Deliver the card to the person.

Words to Know

accident (AK-si-duhnt)—something that is not intended to happen; people sometimes need to forgive someone else for an accident that happened.

enemy (EN-uh-mee)—someone who hates and wants to harm someone else; Corrie ten Boom forgave the people who harmed her family during World War II.

grudge (GRUHJ)—anger toward someone who has hurt or teased you in the past; people who show forgiveness do not hold grudges.

Read More

Doudna, Kelly. *I Am Sorry.* Good Manners. Edina, Minn.: Abdo, 2001.
Kent, Susan. *Learning How to Say You Are Sorry.* The Violence Prevention Library. New York: PowerKids Press, 2001.

Internet Sites

Out on a Limb–A Guide to Getting Along
http://www.urbanext.uiuc.edu/conflict/index.html
Worldwide Forgiveness Alliance
http://www.forgivenessday.org

Index